A COUNTRY DOCTOR

based on the story by
Franz Kafka

Len Jenkin

BROADWAY PLAY PUBLISHING INC
New York
www.broadwayplaypublishing.com
info@broadwayplaypublishing.com

First published by B P P I in June 1999 in the collection *Plays By Len Jenkin*
First printing, this edition: December 2013
I S B N: 978-0-88145-411-6

Book design: Marie Donovan
Page make-up: Adobe Indesign
Typeface: Palatino
Printed and bound in the U S A

ABOUT THE AUTHOR

Len Jenkin's plays include DARK RIDE, TIME IN KAFKA, AMERICAN NOTES, PILGRIMS OF THE NIGHT, CARELESS LOVE, MY UNCLE SAM, LIMBO TALES, PSALM 151, and LIKE I SAY. His works for the stage, often directed by him, have been produced throughout the United States, as well as in England, France, Denmark, Germany and Japan. His adaptations for the stage include Voltaire's CANDIDE (Guthrie Theater, Minneapolis), Aristophanes' THE BIRDS (Yale Repertory Theater, New Haven), and Kafka's A COUNTRY DOCTOR (Classic Stage Company, New York).

His novel *N Judah* is currently available in bookstores and on the web at lenjenkin.com. He has also worked in television and for feature films.

He has received three OBIE awards for Directing and Playwriting, a Guggenheim Fellowship, a Rockefeller Foundation Award, a nomination for an Emmy Award, the Helen Merrill Award, and four National Endowment for the Arts Fellowships.

He teaches in the Dramatic Writing Department, Tisch School of the Arts, New York University.

A COUNTRY DOCTOR was first produced by the Classic Stage Company in New York in 1986. The cast and creative contributors were:

Laura Innes
Olek Krupa
Stephen Mellor
Richard Merrell
Kristine Neilsen
Rochelle Parker
Rocco Sisto

Director .... Lawrence Sacharow
Set design .... Marjorie Kellogg
Lighting .... Arden Fingerhut
Costumes .... Marianne Powell-Parker
Sound .... Tom Gould
Music .... Peter Gordon
Stage manager .... Ricki Grosberg

The setting for A COUNTRY DOCTOR should be simple; the essential people and objects, isolated, with darkness around them. Certain ordinary items should be present: books, tea, doctor's bag, etc. Some objects or set pieces should be an *idea* of that object, rather than a sample of the "real thing." In so many words—like Kafka. The feel should become progressively less ordinary and more otherworldly as the Country Doctor, the Wedding Guest, and Kafka progress on their journeys. Expressive lighting is vital (night, snow, Prague, highway, sickroom, horses, etc). The Country Doctor character is played by various actors and actresses, with specifics as indicated in the text. The PATIENT should be played by an actress. The work can be performed by a company as small as seven.

When in Prague, Klezmer music—when in America, country music from before the sixties, before the Nashville era—musics with some lonesome soul—

And as he went forth, Kartophilus struck him and said, "Go quicker, man." And Jesus replied: "I, indeed, go quickly, but thou shalt tarry till I come again."
Roger of Wendover, *Chronicles of Saint Alban's*, 1216-36

for Joseph K

Scene One

(Empty stage. The PITCHMAN *enters, reaches into his pocket, takes out a small device.)*

PITCHMAN: Ladies and gentlemen, this is what is known as the lookbackoscope. It's imported from Czechoslovakia. This amazing little optical device will do over thirty amazing things, and I would like to amaze you with just a few of them.

If you want to see behind you, you don't have to turn around or let anyone know you're looking. Look through it like this—and see everything going on behind you at all times. Oooooh! In Czechoslovakia the cops use this to catch the robbers, and the robbers use it to watch out for the cops. I guarantee nobody will ever know you're looking.

You wanna see up in that third-floor window? Up there in that secret little room? Don't call the fire department to bring you a ladder—look through the viewer like this—you won't miss a thing! Ooooh!

If you wanna to see around a corner, see where the strange noises are coming from, just hold it like this— you'll see everything, and I mean everything.

Boys, if you're standing on a windy street corner and a pretty girl walks by, anything you see through the lookbackoscope is nobody's business but your own.

Now ladies and gentlemen, these are made to sell for one dollar. I'm sure, if you had one, you wouldn't take a dollar for it. But right now, I'm gonna pass these out for the cost of packing, shipping, handling, and importation alone—twenty-five cents.

Oh, yeah—another special feature! If you hold it to your eye like this and turn it upside down, that's when you see everything upside-down. The boys can see the girls, the girls can see the boys, upside-down on their way to Sunday school on Sunday morning.

(*The* PITCHMAN *holds the lookbackoscope up to his eye. He stares through it.*)

(*In another area, the figure of the* COUNTRY DOCTOR *appears, leaning into the wind and snow.*)

PITCHMAN: Well, whaddaya know. A country doctor. Take a look. Amazing. The things you see when nobody knows you're looking...

Scene Two

(*The* PITCHMAN *is gone. The* COUNTRY DOCTOR *is motionless.*)

ANNOUNCER ONE: *EIN LANDARZT!*

ANNOUNCER TWO: THE COUNTRY DOCTOR!

ANNOUNCER ONE: *(Whisper)* No...*A...EIN LANDARZT!*

ANNOUNCER TWO: *A* COUNTRY DOCTOR!

VOICE OF PATIENT: *(Whisper)* Doctor—let me die.

(*Snow falls on the figure of the* COUNTRY DOCTOR.*)

Scene Three

(A trio of musicians appears, two men and a woman in performance poses. They remain motionless, a waxwork, as music plays. The music ends. The woman and one man remain motionless. The other man, who is the WEDDING GUEST, *steps forward. He looks at his watch.)*

WEDDING GUEST: I'm late for this doctor's appointment, and then I've gotta drive up to the country. Two people I used to work with are getting married. These things happen, right? They must want me there. They invited me. I won't hide. Besides, they love each other. That's what they told me. So, a wedding. I got my tie right here. *(Show tie)* They're having it in their backyard.

(He turns to go, then sees the still motionless duo. He looks quietly at them for a long moment. They leave. He remains. Darkness)

Scene Four

(A doctor's waiting room. A row of very sick PATIENTS. *Among them,* FRANZ KAFKA, *coughing. A* NURSE. *A magazine rack. From offstage, screams)*

PATIENT: What are they doing? Hanging a pig in there, or what?

NURSE: Shhhhhhh.

(The WEDDING GUEST *enters.)*

GUEST: Excuse me. I have an appointment at…

NURSE: Wait here, please. The doctor will be with you in a moment.

GUEST: Uh, I'm in a hurry. Gotta drive up to a wedding. In the country. Don't wanna be late.

NURSE: Wait here, please.

(All PATIENTS *cough harshly.)*

GUEST: These people look awfully sick. Am I in the right…?

NURSE: The doctor also runs a sanitarium in the mountains. T B. Relax. Read a magazine.

(The WEDDING GUEST *sits among the* PATIENTS.*)*

GUEST: Guess I'll read a magazine…

PATIENTS: Shhhhhh! You're disturbing the doctor!

NURSE: Naughty.

GUEST: *(Softer, leafing through magazines) T V Guide*? *Family Circle*?

PATIENT ONE: *Voyeur.*

GUEST: *Guns and Ammo*?

PATIENT TWO: *Voyeur.*

GUEST: *U F O Review*?

PATIENT THREE: *Voyeur*!

GUEST: This magazine is called *Voyeur*. Uh, it's full of color photos of girls. Nothing to read, though. Ah, here's a page with words on it. Letters to *Voyeur*.

(As the GUEST *reads the letter, the* NURSE *and* PATIENTS *listen eagerly, as if to a favorite tale they know by heart.)*

GUEST: Dear Voyeur, I'm a freshman at a midwestern college. I was cruising the motel strip one night after a few beers when I see this blonde chick with her thumb out, wearing a pair of the tightest cutoffs I'd ever seen. My bonger jumped in my Levis as I pulled up and asked where she was going…

NURSE: With you…

GUEST: …she said. I couldn't believe my luck. We pulled into the nearest motel, and as soon as we got in the room, her tongue was down my throat. I thought

I was gonna explode. But then, she pulled away. She said…

NURSE: I need some champagne to really get me in the mood.

GUEST: I remembered a liquor store a few miles back, so I lit out for the car. I bought a couple of bottles of California brut and headed back up the strip. Then I realized, I didn't remember which motel we'd checked into! They flashed by, one after another. I turned around, drove back the other way, hoping something would jog my beer-soaked brain. My dick was dying. Finally, I saw one I thought might be it.

GUEST & PATIENTS: The Blue Spruce!

GUEST: I pulled in, and then I realized…I forgot the room number! The place was quiet as death. I took a guess, knocked on a door. A fat man in a T-shirt opened it. Behind him I could see a woman lying on a bed, reading a magazine. As a matter of fact, it was *Voyeur*. He said…

PATIENT: What the hell do you want?

GUEST: To give you this champagne, I said. I handed it to him, and he took it, and slammed the door in my face. It was almost dawn. I got back in the car. I took off. Now I drive forever up and down the motel strip, looking for that girl, wondering if she's still out there somewhere, waiting for me. The motels flash by, one after another, one after another. Sincerely, a student.

NURSE: The doctor will see you now.

(The DOCTOR *enters.)*

DOCTOR: *(To* GUEST*)* Symptoms?

GUEST: I've been nervous lately—jumpy. I feel like something's…

DOCTOR: Breathe.

(The DOCTOR *examines him. The* GUEST *breathes.)*

DOCTOR: AHA! You're as healthy as an ox! Get out of my office! My time is liniment!

(All PATIENTS *laugh hysterically.)*

GUEST: Don't rub it in!

(All PATIENTS *stare silently at the* GUEST's *attempt at humor. The* GUEST *exits. A bus horn sounds. All* PATIENTS *except* KAFKA *rise and exit.)*

KAFKA: A friend of mine is a doctor, outside of Kierling. He recommends cold baths for the lungs.

DOCTOR: Ridiculous.

KAFKA: Doctor, what do you think of the idea that there is only one disease, no more, and men of medicine chase after it blindly as if hunting a beast in an endless forest.

DOCTOR: Ridiculous.

(Bus horn sounds again.)

DOCTOR: Franz! The bus for the santorium is leav…

KAFKA: I have some personal matters to attend to before I can leave.

DOCTOR: Franz! The pure air of the forest! *(Breathes deeply)* It is absolutely necessary for the success of your treatment that you…

KAFKA: I'll get there.

DOCTOR: Yes, I hope you will.

(The DOCTOR *exits. As* KAFKA *exits, the* NURSE *begins reciting to herself, from memory.)*

NURSE: Dear *Voyeur*, I'm a freshman at a midwestern college. I was cruising the motel strip one night after a few beers when I saw this blonde chick with her thumb out, wearing a pair of the tightest cutoffs I've ever seen.

I couldn't believe my luck. I thought I was going to explode.

(Darkness)

Scene Five

(The GUEST, *looking at his watch)*

GUEST: I had to get upstate to this wedding...

(An older man, in old-fashioned dress, approaches the GUEST. *This is the first version of* THE COUNTRY DOCTOR*)*

GUEST: ...when a man grabs me by the shoulder and starts talking.

DOCTOR: I am the...

GUEST: Hey—not today, hah. I'm already late, and I...

(In another area, lights up on a PATIENT *in bed. On either side of the* PATIENT, *his elderly parents. The* PATIENT *screams in agony.)*

DOCTOR: *(To* GUEST*)* I am the country doctor.

(The DOCTOR's *living room appears. The* DOCTOR *seats himself. He reads. The* WEDDING GUEST *watches.)*

DOCTOR: It began one quiet evening, at home. I was alone.

*(*ROSE, *the* DOCTOR's *housemaid, enters with a tray of tea things, wearing an old-fashioned dress, a black ribbon around her neck.)*

ROSE: Your tea, doctor.

DOCTOR: Except for Rose, an illiterate girl from the village, who lived in, and took care of things.

(The DOCTOR *takes a sip, continues reading, and ignores* ROSE's *questions.)*

ROSE: Not too hot, I hope? Enough cream? Too much cream? It's all right, then? *(With some irony)* Good.

*(*ROSE *exits. A* WEATHERMAN *appears, talking into a radio microphone.)*

WEATHERMAN: Verhaben der schluff von Radio Slovakia. Schnow in Prague. Der barometer is schnell gefallen. Schnow! Efen the elfs in der Black Forest are freezing their little green asses off. Heh-heh-heh. Verhaben grosse schnow. Travel advisories have been posted. Roads are blocked by snow. Travel advisories have been posted.

(The WEATHERMAN *is gone. A phone rings.)*

DOCTOR: The night bell!

(He takes a cell phone out of his pocket.)

DOCTOR: Country Doctor here.

(In the bed area, the PATIENT'S MOTHER *holds a phone to the lips of the* PATIENT. *The* PATIENT *screams in agony. The* MOTHER *takes the phone away, speaks into it.)*

MOTHER: You have to start on an urgent journey. A seriously ill patient is waiting for you in a village ten miles off.

DOCTOR: I'll get there.

MOTHER: It's not that easy. A raging blizzard of snow fills all the wide spaces between us.

(The PATIENT *screams again.)*

MOTHER: Doctor?

DOCTOR: Yes?

MOTHER: Save my child!

(The MOTHER *and* DOCTOR *hang up phones.)*

DOCTOR: *(To* GUEST*)* I was in great perplexity. I had to start on an urgent journey. A seriously ill patient was waiting for me in a village…uh…

FATHER & MOTHER: TEN MILES!

DOCTOR: Ten miles off. A raging blizzard of snow fills all the wide spaces between us. But I have a carriage, light, with big wheels, perfect for our country roads. ROSE!

ROSE: *(Entering)* Yeah?

DOCTOR: My fur! My instrument bag! My rubbers! No! My galoshes!

*(*ROSE *rushes in and out getting everything, then helps to dress the doctor.)*

DOCTOR: Hitch up the horse!

*(*ROSE *runs off. The doctor's living room is gone. Courtyard. Snow.)*

DOCTOR: Muffled in furs, my bag of instruments in my hand, I was in the courtyard, ready to be off!

*(*ROSE *rushes up to the* DOCTOR.*)*

ROSE: The horse is dead.

DOCTOR: My horse had died in the night, worn out by the strain of this icy winter; my housemaid was now running around the village…

*(*ROSE *rushes off.)*

DOCTOR: …trying to borrow a horse. But it was hopeless. I knew it. The patient could be dying and I stood there, more and more covered with snow, more and more unable to move.

(The DOCTOR *is motionless, snow piled on his shoulders. The* GUEST *looks at his watch.)*

GUEST: Look, I don't know why you're telling me all this. I mean, it's not like your life isn't interesting and all, but I've gotta get…

(*A* NARRATOR *appears, along with* ROSE, *who holds a lantern.*)

Scene Six

NARRATOR: (*To* GUEST *and audience*) Sit back and relax. Pop open a beer and watch closely, as we follow Rose down to the village. We all know the village—Home, Sweet Home. Rose's first stop: the 7-Eleven.

(*The* DOCTOR, GUEST *and* NARRATOR *are gone. Bright fluorescent light. Slurpee machine. A* CASHIER. *On the motionless checkout line, everyone is holding a six-pack. A* WOMAN *enters.*)

WOMAN: Hey, Charlie? `Zat you?

(*The last man in line responds.*)

CHARLIE: Yeah.

WOMAN: Haven't seen you for a long time.

CHARLIE: Haven't seen you for a long time.

WOMAN: Three or four months.

CHARLIE: Yeah.

WOMAN: You an Eileen got married, hah?

CHARLIE: Yeah…uh, didn't work out so good…

WOMAN: You get a divorce?

CHARLIE: We're separated.

WOMAN: Yeah?

CHARLIE: Yeah.

WOMAN: Where you living?

CHARLIE: In the van. Broke down over in Burien, spent the whole damn day working on it.

WOMAN: It's running now, hah?

CHARLIE: Yeah. Uh, you come in here to get some smokes?

WOMAN: No.

CHARLIE: What'd you come in here for?

WOMAN: I don't know. I'm just hanging around, you know.

CHARLIE: Yeah. Well, what are you doing? You working?

WOMAN: Yeah. Since Tuesday. I'm gonna tell those unemployment bastards to fuck off. I got this job working for Sandra.

CHARLIE: You working the register?

WOMAN: Naw. I'm in the back. Sandra's my friend, you know. She's trying to help me out. We talk about all kinds of stuff. Not like Arthur and those guys. You know Arthur?

CHARLIE: He the one, his brother's doing five upstate?

WOMAN: Yeah, that's him. Human slime, alla them. That's what they are, you know. He came on to me. God, he was pathetic.

CHARLIE: Anyone who wants someone who doesn't want them is pathetic.

WOMAN: Slime.

CHARLIE: I don't know. I mean, I don't hang out with them, so I don't know.

WOMAN: You know now. I'm telling you.

(ROSE, *holding up her lantern, enters the 7-Eleven.*)

ROSE: Anybody in here got a horse? For the doctor? *(To* WOMAN*)* You got a horse? Somebody's sick. You might be sick someday and what if nobody'd lend your doctor a horse? Then you'd die.

WOMAN: I don't feel too good right now. *(To* CHARLIE*)* I'm living up at 49th and Admiral. Gimme a ride?

(Suddenly the line of customers begins moving rapidly past the CASHIER.*)*

CASHIER: Next!

ROSE: Horse?

CASHIER: Next!

ROSE: Horse?

CASHIER: Next!

ROSE: Horse?

(Everyone is gone but ROSE *and the* CASHIER.*)*

ROSE: *(To* CASHIER*)* Would you lend the doctor a horse?

(The CASHIER *silently exits, and the 7-Eleven is gone.)*

(A NARRATOR *joins* ROSE *as the* COUNTRY DOCTOR *enters. A pigsty. The* GUEST *still watches.)*

NARRATOR: In the gateway Rose appeared, waved her lantern. She was alone.

DOCTOR: *(To* GUEST*)* Of course. Who would lend a horse, at this time of night, for such a journey? I paced the courtyard once more. I could see no way out. In my confused distress, I kicked at the door of the uninhabited pigsty.

(He does so. A GROOM, *filthy horseblanket over his shoulders, emerges from the pigsty.)*

GROOM: Shall I yoke up the horses? They've been fucking in there.

DOCTOR: Who are you? And what are you doing in my uninhabited pigsty?

GROOM: *(Calling into pigsty)* Holla, Brother! Holla, Sister!

(Two "horses" and the DOCTOR's *"carriage" emerge from the pigsty. This construct should have elements of both a car and a horsedrawn carriage. The "horses" eyes might be auto taillights. The doctor must be able to ride in it.)*

DOCTOR: Two horses, enormous creatures with powerful flanks, squeezed out through the doorhole. The groom began to hitch them to the carriage.

ROSE: You never know what you'll find in your own house.

DOCTOR: *(To* ROSE*)* Give him a hand!

NARRATOR: And the willing girl hurried to help the groom with the harnessing. Yet hardly was she beside him when...

(The GROOM *leaps on* ROSE, *pushing her to the ground, tearing at her clothes.* ROSE *screams. The* DOCTOR *hauls the* GROOM *off her.)*

DOCTOR: You beast!

NARRATOR: He yelled.

DOCTOR: Do you want a whipping?

NARRATOR: But at that same moment it dawned on him that the man was a stranger, that he didn't know where he'd come from, and that he was eagerly helping the doctor out when everyone else had failed him.

GROOM: *(To* DOCTOR*)* Everyone else has failed you.

(The DOCTOR *releases the* GROOM.*)*

DOCTOR: As if he knew my thoughts he took no offense at my threat but still busied himself with the horses.

GROOM: *(Pointing to carriage)* Get in.

(The DOCTOR *does so.)*

DOCTOR: But I'll drive. You don't know the way.

GROOM: Of course you'll drive. I'm not coming with you anyway. I'm staying here, with Rose.

(The GROOM *rushes toward* ROSE, *who flees.)*

ROSE: Noooo! Noooo!

DOCTOR: *(From carriage)* Stop! STOP!

(The horses whinny loudly. All freeze. The WEDDING GUEST *looks at his watch.)*

GUEST: Oh, shit…I gotta get moving… *(He rushes off. Darkness)*

(A group of well-dressed citizens of Prague, circa 1920. All hold books and chat. A HOUSEMAID, *serving books)*

HOUSEMAID: *(To audience)* Meanwhile, in Prague, a literary gathering. Small, but lively.

(1920s Prague music. All dance. KAFKA *enters.)*

HOUSEMAID: Having been delayed at his doctor's appointment, Kafka arrives. Late.

*(*KAFKA *seats himself at a table alone, with a drink. The dancing ends. A* MAN *approaches him, sits.)*

MAN: Excuse me for disturbing you, but I have to talk to someone. God, what a night. I've been alone with this girl in the room next door…not a room, really. It's actually a large closet. She's the housemaid. I never noticed her before. She's an…animal. Here, at this fancy party, in the pile of coats on the bed. If anyone should have come in…I mean, our hosts are important people…I think I'm in love. Why, we'll get married. I'll teach her to read and write. Ah…the maid's uniform… the lamplight! I hope you don't mind hearing all this. You're the only one here I can trust. By the way, what's your name?

KAFKA: Franz Kafka, and if you weren't so drunk, you wouldn't be talking about an amorous girl to an obviously sick man, about to leave for a sanitorium, who's sitting alone, drinking schnapps.

MAN: We were in a pile of coats, Franz, fur coats, still reeking of the wet snow, and I kissed her mouth, her ears, her shoulders.

(The literary GUESTS *have crept toward* KAFKA *and the* MAN *and are eavesdropping.* KAFKA *notices and tries to change the subject.)*

KAFKA: *(Loudly)* And what did you say your occupation was?

MAN: I'm a country doctor.

GUEST ONE: *(Leaving)* Goodnight.

GUEST TWO: *(Leaving)* Sleep tight.

GUEST THREE: *(Leaving, to* KAFKA*)* Your work is interesting, but not my cup of tea.

(All are gone but the DOCTOR *and* KAFKA*).*

KAFKA: People seem to be able to disgorge words from their mouths, like huge rats.

(The HOUSEMAID *appears, holding a lantern.)*

KAFKA: *(To audience)* In the vestibule stood the housemaid, to light us down the stairs. Her neck was bare, save for a black velvet ribbon around her throat.

HOUSEMAID: Her cheeks were flushed, for she had drunk some wine. He could see her lips trembling. At the foot of the stairs she put down the lantern, took a step toward the man, embraced him, and remained in the embrace.

(The HOUSEMAID *embraces this version of the country doctor, but speaks to* KAFKA *over his shoulder.)*

HOUSEMAID: Pssst! I've been watching you all night. I've read your stories. You don't impress me at all. Everything you say is boring and incomprehensible, but that alone doesn't make it true.

(*The* HOUSEMAID *shoves them both out into the snow. She's gone.*)

KAFKA: Who is she? Is she the housemaid at all? She looked like a country girl. In the dim light, of course, it was hard to tell, but her face reminded me of… She's very beautiful.

DOCTOR: Who? What are you babbling about?

KAFKA: The housemaid. You should be certain to behave in a…

DOCTOR: Forget about her. You're the only man I can trust. I am the country doctor. I was in great perplexity.

Scene Seven

(ROSE, *the* GROOM, *and another version of the* DOCTOR, *in his carriage, appear. The* GROOM *advances on* ROSE. *She flees, exits.*)

ROSE: Noooooooo!

GROOM: ROSE! ROSE!

DOCTOR: (*At the literary gathering, to* KAFKA) Rose fled into the house. I could see that she put out the lights in the entrance hall and in her further flight darkened all the rooms, one by one, to keep herself from being discovered.

(KAFKA *and the* DOCTOR *speaking to him are gone.*)

DOCTOR: (*In carriage, to* GROOM) You! You're coming with me, or I won't go, urgent as my journey is, I don't intend to pay for it by handing the girl over to you.

GROOM: *(To horses)* GEE UP!

(The "horses" whinny loudly as the carriage begins to move, bearing the DOCTOR away.)

GROOM: ROSE! ROSE!

DOCTOR: STOP! STOP!

(The GROOM rushes off after ROSE. He's gone. Snow. Music, loud and percussive, as the DOCTOR speaks from the moving carriage)

DOCTOR: I could hear the door of my house splinter and burst as the groom charged at it—and then I was deafened and blinded by a snowstorm that buffeted all my senses.

(The carriage comes to a halt. The music stops. A NARRATOR.)

NARRATOR: But this, only for a moment, for as if his courtyard gate opened out directly onto his patient's farmyard, he was already there.

(The bed appears, with the PATIENT in it, and the parents next to it. The PATIENT is played by an actess. A smoking stove)

NARRATOR: The horses stood quietly; the blizzard had stopped; moonlight all around; somewhere in the distance a village choir was singing.

CHOIR: Have no fear of death or pain,
The doctor's come to heal us all,
He's the doctor, he's the doctor.

Have no fear of death or pain,
The doctor's come to heal us all,
He's the doctor, he's the doctor.

NARRATOR: His patient's parents hurried out of the house…

(The NARRATOR *is gone, as the parents rush toward the doctor, draw him toward the bed.)*

FATHER: Ein landarzt!

MOTHER: Thank God.

FATHER: Thank God...

MOTHER: Doctor, save my child!

DOCTOR: In the sickroom, the air was almost unbreathable. The neglected stove was smoking. I wanted to open a window, but first I had to look at my patient.

PATIENT: Doctor. Let me die.

DOCTOR: I glanced around the room. No one else had heard it. The parents were leaning forward in silence, waiting for my verdict. I opened my bag and hunted among my instruments. The patient kept clutching at me.

PATIENT: Doctor, let me die.

(Darkness)

Scene Eight

(The GUEST *appears. He checks his watch.)*

GUEST: Late, dammit. Some people can't seem to stop talking... Been driving for hours. I stopped, got a cup of coffee and some shit to go with it, propped 'em up on the dash. Just hope I don't miss the damn ceremony. Oh, my God! I forgot to get them a present. I'll just tell them what a hurry I was in, I'll tell them some story or other. Guess I'll try the radio. Sometimes these small-town stations have amusing programs.

(Music. Then the GUEST *changes stations. Lights up, in another area, on a woman in an apron,* MAXINE*)*

LOVELINER: *(Radio voice)* You're on the Loveline. First names only.

MAXINE: Maxine.

LOVELINER: Where are you from originally, Maxine?

MAXINE: Right here in Burien.

LOVELINER: Hometown girl, eh. How's the weather up there?

MAXINE: We got a lot of snow. I don't know how I'm gonna get to work tomorrow.

LOVELINER: What kind of work do you do, Maxine?

MAXINE: I'm a nurse.

LOVELINER: How do you like your work, Maxine?

MAXINE: It's O K, I guess.

LOVELINER: Describe yourself for the listeners, Maxine. Height?

MAXINE: Five four.

LOVELINER: Weight?

MAXINE: Well, I'm slimming down. I want to…

LOVELINER: Taking it off, eh. Good. Maxine? Maxine?

MAXINE: Yes.

LOVELINER: You're still on the Loveline. Any hobbies?

MAXINE: I don't collect stamps or anything.

LOVELINER: Now for the big question, Maxine. The kind of man you're looking for.

MAXINE: Uh…well, someone who'd be nice to me. Not much else matters, really.

LOVELINER: Not looks? Tall, dark, and handsome? How about a blond beachboy type?

MAXINE: Well, I'm a little older, you see, and I'd just like someone…

LOVELINER: We know, Maxine. Someone real nice.

MAXINE: I don't mean that.

LOVELINER: O K! Any of you gentlemen out there who like the sound of Maxine, give the Loveliner a call and get her number. Thank you, Maxine. Hello, you're on the Loveline.

(Lights up on the entire cast as they stand quietly, each in their own space. They listen, along with MAXINE *and the* GUEST.*)*

GUEST: On the Loveline.

LOVELINER: Where are you from originally, John? Are you working? How do you like it? How old are you? Hobbies, Jill? Like the outdoors? Sports? Read books, Joe? Any children, Jane? Describe yourself, Bill. Beard? Moustache? Height? Weight? Taking it off, eh. Good. Tell us the kind of girl you're looking for, Franz. Age? Type? Smoker O K? Blonde? Brunette? Occasional social drinker O K? Children O K? Where are you from originally, Franz? This is the Loveline, the Loveline, the Loveline. This is the Loveliner on the Loveline. Call in, call out, call around, it's out there, you'll find it, don't give up…

(All walk slowly offstage, leaving only the WEDDING GUEST *and the* PITCHMAN.*)*

Scene Nine

(The PITCHMAN *begins hitchhiking. A* NARRATOR *appears.)*

NARRATOR: Before he knew it, the Wedding Guest stopped for a hitchhiker by the side of the road. The man got in.

(The NARRATOR *is gone. The* PITCHMAN *moves next to the* GUEST.*)*

PITCHMAN: Wedding, eh? A beautiful occasion.

GUEST: Yeah, it's in the country.

PITCHMAN: How fortunate. Exactly where I'm headed.

GUEST: You know, we used to play music. The three of us.

PITCHMAN: Jealous, eh? Bride must be a looker. My first wife was a beauty. She got lost in a blizzard. After a while, I never missed her.

GUEST: It's funny how…I mean, I…

PITCHMAN: What are you babbling about?

GUEST: Nothing. To top it off, I'm late. I could miss the whole damn ceremony.

PITCHMAN: I doubt it. In fact, you're right on time, and to thank you properly for helping me continue my travels at a rather low moment in my career, I'm gonna give you some advice, advice gained through a lifetime, yours for the pleasure of your company, and the effort of attention. DON'T LISTEN TO CRAZY STORIES.

ANNOUNCER ONE: *EIN LANDARZT!*

ANNOUNCER TWO: THE COUNTRY DOCTOR!

ANNOUNCER ONE: No! *A. EIN LANDARZT!*

ANNOUNCER TWO: A COUNTRY DOCTOR!

PITCHMAN: I believe you're in the market for a wedding gift. I happen to have here a little device known in Czechoslovakia as the Lookbackoscope. Pull over. Pull over and take a look. Usually sells for a dollar. I've seen some funny things through here. Movie starlets disrobing! Views of Prague!

GUEST: Hey—this ain't gonna be a story about some doctor, 'cause if it is, I'm not…

PITCHMAN: Take a look! You'll see a small room, stuffy. Outside the window, snow. You're right on time. Take this.

(The PITCHMAN *hands the* GUEST *a doctor's instrument bag, and he's gone.)*

Scene Ten

(The bed, and in it the PATIENT, *and alongside it, the* PATIENT'*s parents. The* MOTHER *rushes up to the* GUEST *and drags him toward the* PATIENT.*)*

MOTHER: Doctor, praise God you're here. Save my child.

PATIENT: Doctor! Let me die.

DOCTOR: The mother stood by the bedside and cajoled me toward the patient.

MOTHER: Cajole! Cajole!

(The GUEST/DOCTOR *goes forward to the bed, examines the* PATIENT.*)*

DOCTOR: *(To audience)* This child is not dying—far from it. Something a little wrong with the circulation, covered up too heavily by doting parents, but fine, and best thrown out of bed with one shove. I am no world reformer, and so I let the patient lie. *(To parents)* Just a touch of flu. This icy winter. Rest. Fluids.

(The parents stare at the doctor in disbelief. The MOTHER *weeps on the* FATHER'*s shoulder.)*

DOCTOR: What more could I do? The child seemed fine. I picked up a pair of tweezers, examined them in the lamplight, and laid them down again. It's only in pointless cases like this that the gods choose to be helpful; send the missing horses, even a groom—and only now did I remember Rose again—

(The GROOM *and* ROSE *appear in another area.)*

GROOM: Rose! ROSE!

ROSE: Nooooooo!

(She flees, he follows, they're gone.)

DOCTOR: How could I pull her out from under that groom at ten miles' distance, with a team of horses I couldn't control. These horses, now, they had somehow slipped the reins, pushed open the window from the outside, and stood eyeing the patient.

(The "horses" do so, i.e., some portion of the horses/carriage construct pushes into the room. Loud whinnys)

DOCTOR: Better go home at once, I thought, as if the horses were summoning me to the return journey.

FATHER: Doctor, are you all right?

(The FATHER *hands the* DOCTOR *a drink.)*

DOCTOR: The old man clapped me on the shoulder, a familiarity justified by this offer of his schnapps. In the narrow confines of the old man's thoughts I felt ill.

NARRATOR: *(O S)* Imagine what he's thinking!

FATHER: If God were to listen to the prayers of buzzards, there'd be dead horses lying about everywhere.

(The horses whinny loudly, then quiet.)

DOCTOR: *(To audience)* I am the district doctor and do my duty to the point where it becomes almost too much. I'm badly paid, and yet I'm generous, helpful to the poor. I still had to see that Rose was all right, and then the child might have its way…

PATIENT: *(Softly)* Doctor, let me die.

DOCTOR: …and I wanted to die too. What was I doing there in that endless winter? My horse was dead, and not one person in the village would lend me another.

I had to pull my team out of the pigsty. If they hadn't chanced to be horses, I should have had to travel with swine. That was how it was. And I nodded to the family. They knew nothing about it, and if they had known, they wouldn't have believed it. To write prescriptions is easy, but to come to an understanding with people is hard.

ALL: To write prescriptions is easy, but to come to an understanding with people is hard.

(Darkness)

Scene Eleven

(1920s Prague music. KAFKA's FATHER, *in bed, invisible under a pile of covers.* KAFKA *enters.)*

NARRATOR: Meanwhile, in Prague, Franz visits his father.

KAFKA: *(To himself)* To write prescriptions is easy, but to come to an understanding with people is hard.

NARRATOR: He leans over the bed and arranges the covers.

*(*KAFKA *does so as the* NARRATOR *exits.)*

KAFKA: Father, it's dark in here.

FATHER: Yes. It's dark enough.

KAFKA: You've shut the window too. The air is almost unbreathable.

FATHER: I prefer it like that.

KAFKA: Father, I'm leaving today for a sanitorium in the mountains. They say it will help my…

FATHER: Am I well covered up now? Am I well covered up?

KAFKA: Don't worry. You're well covered up.

FATHER: NO! You want to cover me up, my rotten, twisted, stunted little darling, but I'm far from being covered up yet! Even if this is the last strength I have, it's enough for you. You went to all the literary gatherings, didn't you? Small, but lively.

(1920s Prague dance music, and gone)

FATHER: And there, she lifted up her skirts, like this!

(KAFKA's FATHER rises up in bed, his head and body still concealed by the covers—a ghostly figure. He demonstrates the skirt lifting.)

FATHER: The nasty little goose! Because she lifted up her skirts like this, and this, you made up to her with all your silly talk, and in order to satisfy yourself with her undisturbed you have stuck your father into bed so that he can't move! But he can move, can't he? You think life is a thing in your head. You can't face the next moment, and yet you don't kill yourself but foolishly struggle to go on living. You pretend to help me in my agony, but you never do enough.

(The ghostly figure rises, moves off the bed toward KAFKA.)

FATHER: Till this moment you've only known about yourself. Now you know what else there is in the world. An innocent child, yes, that you were, but you have become a devilish human being! And, therefore, take note: I sentence you now to death by…

VOICE OF KAFKA'S MOTHER: Franz! Your father's been dead for ten years, and I'm the girl that knows.

KAFKA: *(Looking around)* Mother?

(KAFKA's FATHER dies, collapsing in a pile of empty bedclothes.)

VOICE OF KAFKA'S MOTHER: He's wandering forever in the other world, baby, and if you want him to take a strap to you, you'll have to chase him through the boneyard. You ain't smart enough to blow your own nose—but, you never were. You're pulling your own poo-poo. Get it?

Scene Twelve

(Lights up on the GUEST*)*

GUEST: I get it…I think. *(Looks at watch)* Hopeless. They're probably in the middle of the wedding march by now. By the way, that hitchhiker stole my car. I am now travelling to this wedding in the cab of a large Mac truck.

(Music. A TRUCK DRIVER *joins the guest. The* WOMAN *from the music trio appears in another space, motionless. As the music fades, she's gone.)*

TRUCK DRIVER: Wedding, eh?

GUEST: Yeah. They're having it in their backyard.

TRUCK DRIVER: They live in the country?

GUEST: Yeah.

TRUCK DRIVER: I hate the country. Birds and bees and all that shit. Last summer my wife gets me to drive up to the Cape. Her brother's got a place near Brewster, which is a grocery by a stop sign, and the house is ten miles from there in a buncha sand. I'm there two hours and they're all talking and kidding around, and I'm getting nervous.

(The TRUCK DRIVER'S WIFE *and relatives enter, partying.)*

TRUCK DRIVER: *(To* WIFE*)* I can't stand it up here. I gotta have lights and people.

WIFE: Whattaya think these are, hah? They're not people?

(The relatives freeze in party poses.)

TRUCK DRIVER: All right. I'll stay.

(*The relatives exit, partying. The* WIFE *remains.*)

TRUCK DRIVER: (*To* GUEST) Two-thirty a.m. I wake up in a cold sweat. Fuckin' big green thing is buzzing on the window screen, trying to get in. I look at my wife's face while she's sleeping. Shes still beautiful, you know, real pretty. The thing in the window buzzes again. I gotta leave there.

WIFE: You gotta, you gotta. I don't want you here nervous. But I don't wanna see your face again till you come back to drive us home.

(*The* WIFE *is gone.*)

TRUCK DRIVER: So I get in the car and start driving back to the city. And I get off the highway near Buzzard's Bay, and there's an all night-diner, and I get a cup of coffee and some shit to go with it, and prop 'em up on the dash, and I figure that'll get me through. You know that stretch of highway past Providence where there's no lights, no houses, no nothing? I'm driving there, and I'm driving, and it seems like I'm not getting anywhere, 'cause there's still nothing out there, you know. I feel funny, and all of a sudden I'm thinking that the world's gone, and I'm alone, and I can't tell if that's bad or good or what—and then I see this red light flashing in the mirror and I'm thinking O K, it's four A M and I'm falling out—just gimme the fucking ticket and let me drive away. He comes over to the window and says…

COP: I see guys like you come through here all the time. I expect you, about this time of night, always with the coffee on the dash. Just the right time to tell you a story. "I was in great perplexity. I had to start on an urgent journey. A seriously…" Heh-heh-heh. Sound familiar?

TRUCK DRIVER: I'll wait back by the trailer. I know the damn story by heart. *(He exits.)*

COP: Of course, the first examination of the patient is over by now…

Scene Thirteen

(The PATIENT in bed, and the parents and DOCTOR gathered around. The GUEST watches.)

DOCTOR: *(To parents)* Just a touch of flu. This icy winter. Rest. Fluids. *(To audience)* Well, this should be the end of my visit. I had once more been called out needlessly. I was used to that. The whole district makes my life a torment with my night bell. But that I should have to sacrifice Rose, the beautiful girl who lived in my house for years, almost without my noticing her—that sacrifice is too much to ask. I picked up my bag and reached for my fur.

MOTHER: *(Pointing to FATHER)* The father, sniffing at the glass of schnapps in his hand, frightened, disappointed…

FATHER: *(Pointing to MOTHER)* The mother, biting her lips, with tears in her eyes, fluttering a blood-soaked towel…

(The MOTHER throws the towel at the DOCTOR's feet.)

NARRATOR: *(O S)* Imagine what she's thinking.

MOTHER: Even a blind dog sometimes finds something…

DOCTOR: What do people expect? I went toward the bed again, and this time—the patient welcomed me, smiling.

(The horses whinny loudly.)

DOCTOR: The noise, I suppose, was ordained by heaven to assist the examination—and this time I discovered that the child was indeed ill. In the right side, near the hip, was an open wound, as big as my palm—rose red, dark in the hollows, lighter at the edges, softly granulated, with uneven clots of blood. That was how it looked from a distance. On closer inspection, there was another complication. Worms, as thick and long as my little finger, rose red and blood-spotted, with small white heads and many little legs, were wriggling from the darkness in the interior of the wound, up toward the light. Poor child, you were past helping. I had discovered your great wound. This blossom in your side will destroy you.

(Darkness)

Scene Fourteen

(KAFKA *on a cellphone. A* WOMAN KAFKA *knows talks into a microphone.*)

KAFKA: Yes. Yes, I know I'm a hypochondriac. I'm also actually ill.

WOMAN: That isn't funny, Franz. *(Silence)* Franz?

KAFKA: Yes.

WOMAN: I believe you. But you could be treated here. We'd be together. I could…

KAFKA: No. I would die there.

WOMAN: Don't talk like that.

KAFKA: Why not? I'm quite ready for whatever may come to me. Not because I've done everything that was given me to do. It's because I've done none of it and never can hope to do any of it.

(The WOMAN *steps away from the microphone and stands quietly, head bowed.)*

KAFKA: Please don't come to visit me. Don't call. And don't write.

*(*KAFKA *puts the phone away.)*

Scene Fifteen

(Music. The WOMAN *is gone. The* PITCHMAN *enters, along with an* EXHIBITOR, *who has a large jar of green fluid on a stand.)*

NARRATOR: Franz, on his way to the sanitorium in the mountains, passes a small carnival on the outskirts of Prague. He overhears an interesting conversation. *(*NARRATOR *exits.)*

PITCHMAN: *(To* EXHIBITOR*)* The ability to treat ordinary subjects in a grand manner, to invent tinselled and impressive lies about them, and the gall to sell tickets to their exhibition qualify a man for the showman's trade.

(The PITCHMAN *takes out a two-headed rubber doll.)*

PITCHMAN: Example: A two-headed rubber doll generates little interest on its own. But immersed in a specimen jar of greenish fluid and unveiled during a solemn lecture. *(He plunges the doll into the jar of green fluid.)*

PITCHMAN: …it attracts attention.

EXHIBITOR: This pitiful little person was born just thirty-seven miles from Los Alamos, New Mexico, exactly eight months and three weeks after a huge atomic blast!

PITCHMAN: That's the way to sell 'em, son. And it's the truth. People suffer. You can see the flames in their eyes.

KAFKA: I agree.

PITCHMAN: Do you now?

KAFKA: We human beings should stand before one another with as much sympathy and as much love as if we stood before the gates of hell.

PITCHMAN: My friend, people do suffer—endlessly—except for certain lively moments of relief.

(*At a gesture from the* PITCHMAN, *the* PATIENT *in bed, parents by him, stove, etc, reappears. They are still: waxworks. The* PITCHMAN *guides* KAFKA *toward them.* KAFKA *steps hesitantly into the waxwork, the* PITCHMAN *placing him carefully in the "doctor" position. The* PITCHMAN *returns to the* EXHIBITOR.)

PITCHMAN: *(To audience and* EXHIBITOR*)* The advantage of an exhibit show over an animal show is that exhibits are not alive. Thus, the operator has the security of knowing that his attraction won't die before the season's over. Another advantage of exhibit shows is that they can appeal to the customer's appetite for the morbid and sensational. Exhibits of execution, torture—as well as subjects of a sexy or religious nature are ideal for the exhibit showman. The story of the country doctor is always popular...

(*The* PATIENT *in bed, the parents by him, and* KAFKA *as the* DOCTOR *remain still: waxworks.)*

EXHIBITOR: Ladies and gentlemen: the first lot of figures to which I will call your attention represents a country doctor and his patient. The figure on your right is the country doctor; on the left, the patient. As you know from history, when a country doctor gets to a patient, he bends over the bed, looking as serious as possible.

(KAFKA *does so.*)

EXHIBITOR: In our waxworks, you have a correct representation of the scene, exactly as it happened.

(*The* PITCHMAN *and the* EXHIBITOR *are gone.*)

Scene Sixteen

(*The figures stir…*)

DOCTOR: Poor boy, you were past helping. I had discovered your great wound. This blossom in your side will destroy you. The family was pleased. They saw me busying myself. The mother told the father…

MOTHER: (*To* FATHER) The doctor is at work.

DOCTOR: The father told several guests who were coming in through the moonlight at the open door.

(*Several guests enter, walking on tiptoe, keeping their balance with outstretched arms. One of them is a* CHOIRMASTER.)

FATHER: (*To* GUESTS) The doctor is at work. The doctor is at work.

PATIENT: (*To* DOCTOR) Will you save me?

DOCTOR: (*To audience*) That is what people are like in my district. Always demanding the impossible from the doctor. They have lost the old beliefs. The priest sits at home and unravels his robes, one after another, but the doctor should be able to save everyone with his merciful surgeon's hands. Well, as they wish. I have not offered myself—but if they misuse me for sacred ends, I let that happen to me too. What better do I want, country doctor that I am, robbed of my housemaid, Rose, that beautiful girl who lived in my…

(*The parents and the* CHOIRMASTER *and* GUESTS *advance menacingly toward the* DOCTOR/KAFKA.)

CHOIRMASTER: And so they came toward him, the family and the village elders. Led by the school choirmaster, they sang these words to an utterly simple tune.

(As they sing the following, they tear at the DOCTOR's *clothes, beginning to remove them. He makes no resistance.)*

ALL: *(Singing, except the* DOCTOR*)*
Strip his clothes off, then he'll heal us
If he doesn't, kill him dead!
Only a doctor, only a doctor.

Strip his clothes off, then he'll heal us
If he doesn't, kill him dead!
Only a doctor, only a doctor.

(Darkness)

Scene Seventeen

(The WEDDING GUEST, *alone. He is moving with a gliding motion.)*

WEDDING GUEST: I'll get there. The wedding's close. I can hear the cocktail chatter. It's all right. I can handle it. "Bless you both, and be as happy as you can." *(Looking ahead)* Out there, in the distance, is that a crowd in wedding dresses, tuxedos? There are jugglers, clowns! I'll be there on time. These stories about the doctor take no time at all, actually. Instantaneous. *(Looks at watch)* In fact, I'm early. Think I'll stop and grab a bite. By the way, that trucker dropped me in the middle of nowhere. But I'm now on some kind of moving walkway, lined with shops. Ah...there's a place. The Sign of The Blind Pig: Espresso, Cappuccino.

(The Cafe, Sign of the Blind Pig, appears. A WAITRESS. *A* NARRATOR.*)*

GUEST: I go in, and there's this girl, a waitress or something. She's spraying the pastry counter with Windex, I mean the glass, you know. She's working, and she's a little bored, and a little self-absorbed…

NARRATOR: Imagine what she's thinking!

WAITRESS: I'm Rochelle, and I'm thinking interesting things about myself in a Holiday Inn. There's this man with a sort of bird's head, near the ice machine. I'm on the fifth floor. Uh-oh. Now I'm on the sixth floor.

(The WAITRESS *begins coughing harshly.*)

NARRATOR: T B. Her name is actually Rosa…

GUEST: Is she from Czechos…

NARRATOR: No, you're wrong there. She's Cuban. She's very clever, isn't she?

(The NARRATOR *is gone. The* WAITRESS *leads a young* MAN *and a young* WOMAN *to a table near the* GUEST.)

GUEST: A man and a woman slide into the booth behind me. I can hear every word…

WOMAN: Friend of mine, Charlie Rothstein, took himself off to the High Sierra at the age of twenty to spend his life in meditation, love of God, and meaningful poverty. Beautiful guy. Had a good word to say about every visitor to his little shack. Lived there for ten years, one of the most enlightened beings on the planet.

MAN: Yeah.

WOMAN: Drank nothing but water, ate berries growing wild. His skin was as white as milk.

MAN: Yeah.

WOMAN: Age of thirty, just on the day he was to return to the world of men and teach them how to be like him, he got bit by a rattlesnake. He was sitting soaking up the bliss divine, and that snake just wriggled up and bit him. Big diamondback. He died right there. After twitching in pain for a few hours. His students found him when they drove up that evening, body twisted up horrible as you please.

MAN: Yeah.

WAITRESS: *(Delivering their drinks)* Uh-oh. Now I'm on the seventh floor. *(She exits.)*

WOMAN: Friend of mine, Brian Soapstone, became one of the major cocaine dealers in the city. Went to all the parties, had a taste for tall women with a lot of leg, and little Mexican boys. Had him this Chinese cook made food so good you couldn't believe it. You just sat there in his living room on a furry cushion and never wanted to leave. Brian knew all about art, sex, sports, good skier, one of the nicest guys you'd ever want to meet. He carried on like this for ten years.

MAN: Yeah.

WOMAN: Then his kidneys started to go bad on him. Hadda go in the hospital, and they took one out, and then they told him he hadda stop everything, and Brian told the doctors he wanted to live, and he'd die when he'd die, and a few months later he was back in the hospital. He was dying there for three days. We all went to see him. They couldn't do a thing for him. Dead at thirty. So lemme tell you. Brian paid attention to the outside and forgot the inside. Charlie paid attention to the inside and forgot the outside. Things took charge, and they ain't here no more.

MAN: Yeah.

(The couple rises, ready to go.)

WOMAN: Then, of course, there's the story of the country doctor. "I was in great perplexity" and so on. By this time, his clothes are stripped off him.

Scene Eighteen

(The Sign of the Blind Pig and its customers are gone. We return to the sickroom, with the CHOIRMASTER, *village elders, parents,* PATIENT *in bed, and a* COUNTRY DOCTOR. *The* DOCTOR *is now stripped to a pair of undershorts.)*

ALL: *(Singing softly, except* DOCTOR*)*
Strip his clothes off, then he'll heal us
If he doesn't, kill him dead!
Only a doctor, only a doctor.

DOCTOR: I looked at the people quietly, fingers in my beard, my head cocked to one side. I was altogether composed and equal to the situation, and remained so, although it was no help to me. They laid me down in the bed, on the side of the wound.

(They do so, placing him in bed next to the PATIENT *and exit.* DOCTOR *and* PATIENT *alone in bed.)*

DOCTOR: Then they all left the room. The singing stopped. Clouds covered the moon. The bedding was warm around me.

PATIENT: You know, I have very little confidence in you. You were only blown in here, you didn't come on your own two feet. Instead of helping me, you're cramping me in my deathbed. What I'd like best is to scratch your eyes out.

DOCTOR: You're right. It is a shame. And yet, I am a doctor. What am I to do? Believe me, it's not easy for me either.

PATIENT: Am I supposed to forgive you?

(The PATIENT *shoves the* DOCTOR *roughly out of bed. He tumbles to the floor alongside.)*

PATIENT: Am I supposed to be satisfied with that apology? —But I must be. I can't help it. It's all you have to give me. You know, I always have to put up with things. All I brought into this world is a magnificent wound—it's my sole inheritance.

(The DOCTOR *kneels alongside the bed.)*

DOCTOR: Your mistake is, you don't have a wide enough view. I have been in all the sickrooms, and I tell you: Your wound is not so bad. Done in a tight corner with two strokes of the ax. Many a patient bares his side—and can hardly hear the ax off in the snowy forest, far less that it is coming nearer, and then does not even know it is cutting away at him, day after day.

ALL: *(Offstage voices)* Is that really so?

PATIENT: Or are you deluding me in my fever?

DOCTOR: It is really so. Take the word of honor of an official doctor.

NARRATOR'S VOICE: And the patient took it and lay still.

(The DOCTOR *climbs back in bed alongside the* PATIENT. *Darkness)*

Scene Nineteen

(1920s Prague music. A group of T B PATIENTS, *among them* KAFKA, *enter. A picnic outing. They seat themselves on the ground. A* NURSE *supervises.)*

NURSE: Meanwhile, in a T B sanitorium in the mountains, Franz remembers something that doesn't seem, at the moment, to be part of *A Country Doctor* but is getting mixed up with it in his head. He tells the other patients.

KAFKA: I am a much younger man, about twenty. I am in a village by a river. There's a hotel, and I hear the sound of violins. I sit on a bench by the shore in a twisted position. On the other side of the river are cloudlike mountains. A girl my age sits down alongside me. She has brown hair, and a stray tendril curls at her temple. We talk. I am so close to her I can see the whirl of her right ear, the intricate filigree of her silver earring. I think: Why isn't she constantly amazed by herself? She invites me home, a shabby house nearby. It is early evening. I am sitting with her and her elderly mother in a dark kitchen. We are drinking sweet wine and eating potatoes. Suddenly it starts to snow very heavily outside. Thunder, and the lights flicker, and I see both their faces very clearly in the dim light. The girl smiles.

PATIENT ONE: That's it? That's the story?

KAFKA: Yes. That was how it was.

OTHER PATIENTS: Booooo! Booooo!

NURSE: I have one. I'm a freshman at a midwestern college. I was cruising the motel strip one night after a few beers when I see this chick with her… *(And continuing this story [the GUEST's speech from pages 4-5] very softly under the following:)*

KAFKA: I find that my social or romantic life is often an effort to maintain my sanity by seeing a solid reflection of myself in someone else's eyes…to believe that somebody's home inside me, that person who's there for others, but who I only feel as my invention…and yet there is someone, down there in the dark. If he rose up, he would shine into all these lost forms that drift out of me, turn them into bright messengers…

NURSE: *(Voice rising)* …waiting for me, the motels flash by, one after another… Sincerely, a student.

(A bus horn sounds. All patients, except a WOMAN and KAFKA, rise and exit. That WOMAN takes a step away.)

KAFKA: Stay with me.

WOMAN: I'm not leaving you.

KAFKA: But I am leaving you.

NURSE: The doctor will see you now.

Scene Twenty

(Lights up on a DOCTOR *and the* PATIENT *in bed. The* PATIENT *rests quietly. The* DOCTOR *slides out from under the covers, stands. He is still in his undershorts. This final* DOCTOR *is once again the* WEDDING GUEST. KAFKA *watches.)*

DOCTOR: It was time to think of saving myself. The horses were still standing faithfully in their places. I didnt want to waste time dressing; if the horses raced home as fast as they had come, I should only be springing, as it were, out of this bed into my own.

(The horses whinny loudly. The DOCTOR *rushes to the carriage.)*

DOCTOR: I threw my instrument bag into the carriage; my fur missed its mark—caught on a hook by the sleeve. Good enough. I swung myself in. *(He does so.)*

DOCTOR: GEE UP!

(Music, loud and percussive. The carriage begins to move, very slowly. The DOCTOR *speaks from the moving carriage.)*

DOCTOR: But there was no galloping. Slowly, like old men, we crawled through the desert of snow; behind us echoed a new but mistaken song of the choirmaster and the village elders.

ALL: *(Singing, except* DOCTOR*)*
O be joyful, all you patients,
The doctors laid in bed beside you!

O be joyful, all you patients,
The doctors laid in bed beside you!

DOCTOR: Never shall I reach home at this rate. My blossoming practice is done for. In my house the disgusting groom is raging—Rose is his victim. I do not want to think about it anymore. Naked, exposed to the frost of this unhappy age, I wander astray. My fur is hanging from the back of the carriage, but I cannot reach it, and none of my limber pack of patients lifts a finger. Betrayed! A false alarm on night bell, once answered—it cannot be made good, not ever.

ALL: *(Singing , except* DOCTOR*)*
O be joyful, all you patients,
The doctor's laid in bed beside you!

O be joyful, all you patients,
The doctor's laid in bed beside you!

Scene Twenty-one

(The wedding. A MINISTER, *a* BRIDE *and* GROOM. *Various guests, including* KAFKA. *In another space, the* PATIENT *in bed.)*

(The carriage comes to a halt. The WEDDING GUEST *gets out, takes a step toward the wedding party.)*

MINISTER: I now pronounce…I now pronounce…I…

(Snow falls as we hear the following voices from the group.)

A DOCTOR: I am the country doctor. I was in great perplexity.

PITCHMAN: Look through the viewer like this. You'll see everything, and I mean everything.

ROSE: You never know what you'll find in your own house.

ANOTHER DOCTOR: That was how it was.

KAFKA: To write prescriptions is easy, but to come to an understanding with people is hard.

WEDDING GUEST: I do not want to think about it anymore.

(The PATIENT *leaves the bed and moves to center stage.)*

PATIENT: You do not need to leave your room. Just lie in your bed and listen. Do not even listen, simply wait. Do not even wait, be quite still and solitary. The world will freely offer itself to you to be unmasked. It has no choice. It will roll in ecstasy at you feet.

ANNOUNCER ONE: *EIN LANDARZT*.

ANNOUNCER TWO: A COUNTRY DOCTOR.

(Darkness)

END OF PLAY

www.ingramcontent.com/pod-product-compliance
Lightning Source LLC
Chambersburg PA
CBHW070034110426
42741CB00035B/2767